TONYA C. GEORGE

BEYOND THE CLOUDS

LLC

BEYOND THE CLOUDS

Copyright © 2020 by Tonya C. George

Published by NoonieLand, LLC
Murphy, Texas
www.BeyondTheCloudsBook.com

ISBN: 978-1-7335824-2-1 (Paperback)

Library of Congress Control Number: 2020908594
Names: George, Tonya C., author
Title: Beyond The Clouds / Tonya C. George
Publisher's Note: This is an original work.

Printed in the United States of America

Dedicated to all of God's children.

This book belongs to:

_____

Beyond the clouds
Way past the sky

Above the birds
That fly so high

Beyond the trees
So green and wide

There lives my God
He is my guide

Beyond the clouds
And stars so bright

He gave the moon
To light the night

Beyond the sun
And birds that sing

Yes, Jesus Christ Is King of Kings

Beyond the clouds
He shows me love

A love that's free
Free as a dove

Beyond the land
And grass that grows

He is so wise
He always knows

Beyond the clouds
He hears my prayers

He gives us grace
Because He cares

Beyond each breath
He gives us air

Our God is good
He's everywhere

Beyond
the clouds

Beyond
our eyes

Beyond
the noise

Beyond
the cries

Beyond
this world

And what
we see

There lives
my God

FOOD DONATIONS
FOR THE NEEDY

He lives in me

1) Where does Jesus live?

2) Draw a picture of heaven.

1) What does Jesus do for you?

2) Draw a picture of Jesus.

THE END

www.NoonieLand.com

CPSIA information can be obtained
at www.ICGtesting.com
Printed in the USA
LVHW070430151120
671611LV00010B/475